Love & Peace
COLORING
BOOK

Love & Peace
COLORING
BOOK

THUNDER BAY
P · R · E · S · S
San Diego, California

Thunder Bay Press
An imprint of Printers Row Publishing Group
10350 Barnes Canyon Road, Suite 100, San Diego, CA 92121
www.thunderbaybooks.com • mail@thunderbaybooks.com

Correspondence regarding the content of this book should be sent to Thunder Bay Press, Editorial Department, at the above address. Author and rights inquiries should be sent to Arcturus Holdings Limited, 26/27 Bickels Yard, 151-153 Bermondsey Street, London SE1 3HA, England; info@arcturuspublishing.com.

Thunder Bay Press
Publisher: Peter Norton
Associate Publisher: Ana Parker
Editor: Dan Mansfield
Senior Product Manager: Kathryn C. Dalby

ISBN: 978-1-64517-440-0
CH008219NT

Printed in China

24 23 22 21 20 1 2 3 4 5

Introduction

When you need time for yourself and want to focus your mind on the best in life, what could be more appealing than coloring a set of images that focus on themes of love and peace?

Artist Nina Taylor has created a set of more than 100 detailed pictures that seek to inspire a sense of inner peace and feelings of love. She's included classic symbols of peace like doves, watery creatures like Chinese carp and seahorses, and images of meditation. Hearts and flowers are used in unusual ways, and images such as hamsas and mandalas take in inspiration from other cultures.

Find yourself a quiet spot, your home or outside (if that's where you feel most at peace, and the weather allows), take your colored pencils, pens, or crayons, and turn these beautiful black-and-white outlines into fabulous color pictures.

Choose a color scheme that reflects your feelings at the time—perhaps a soothing pastel palette to achieve calm—or in contrast, vivid colors that burst with warmth to bring your chosen picture to vibrant life.

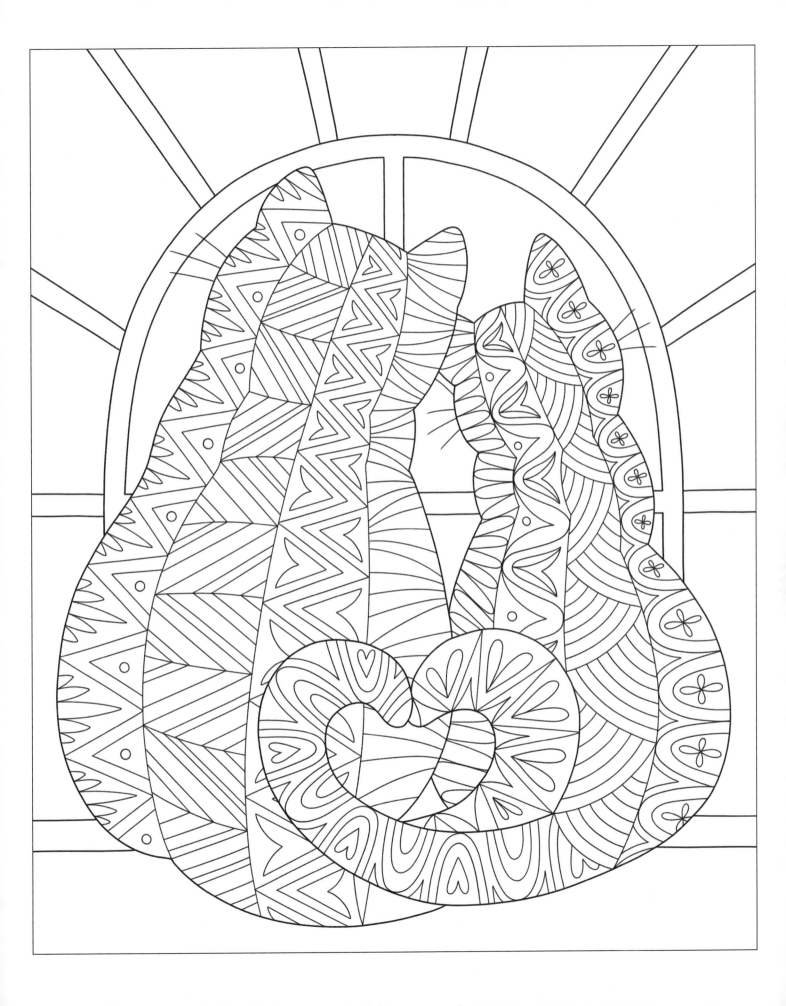

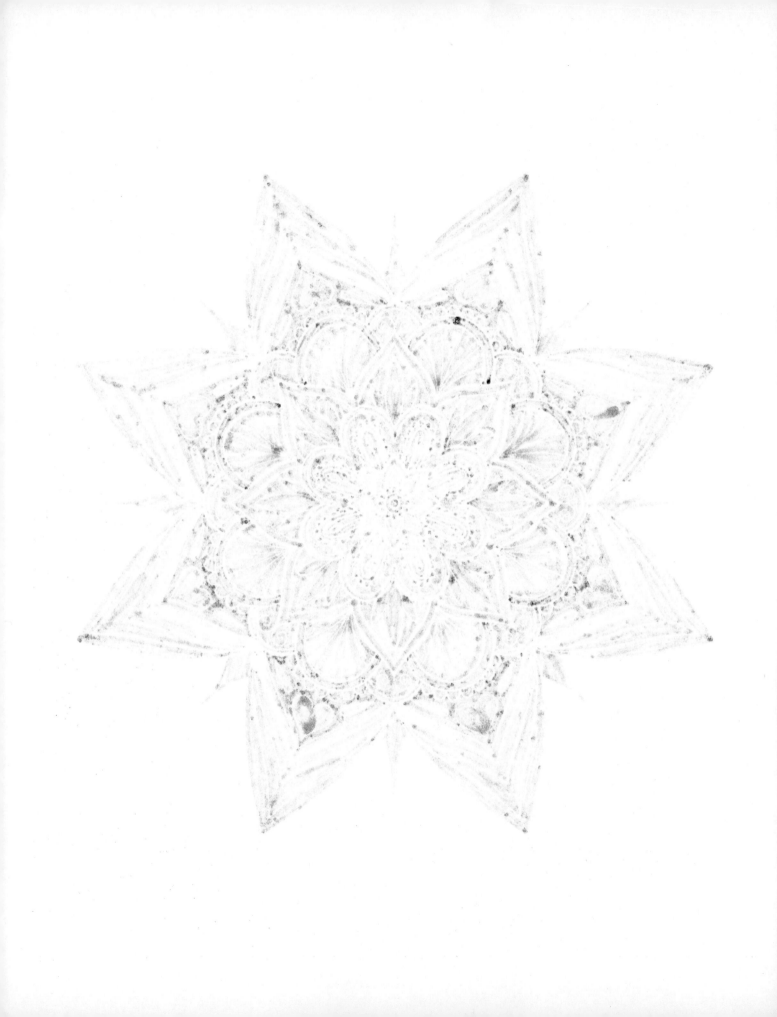

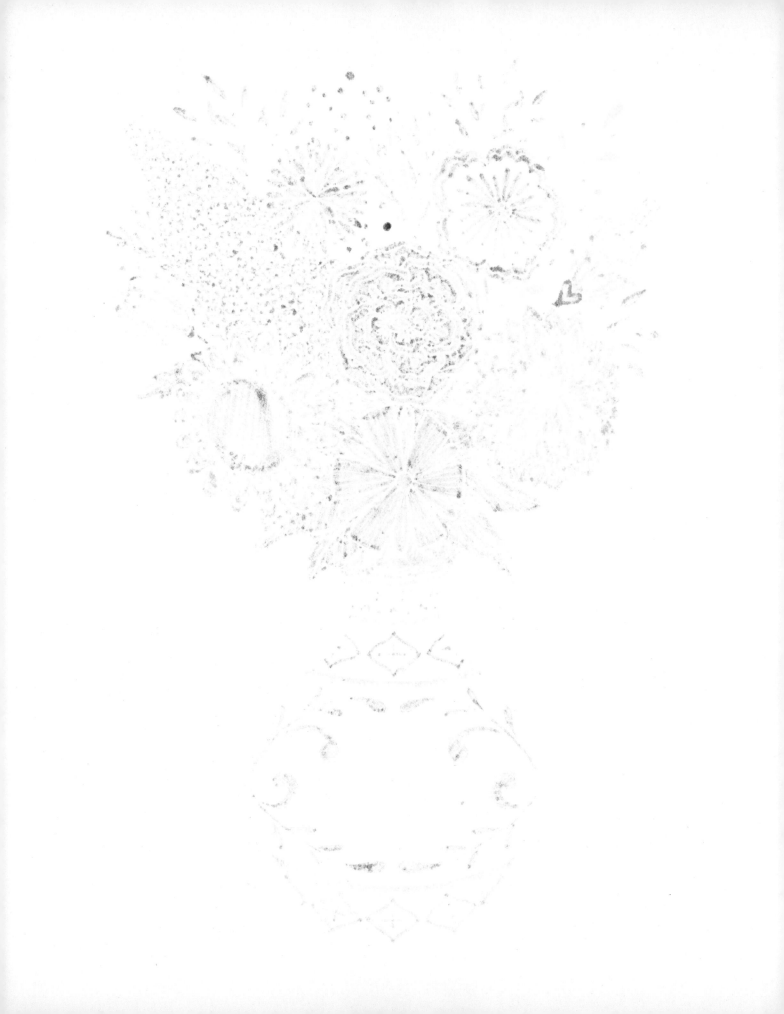

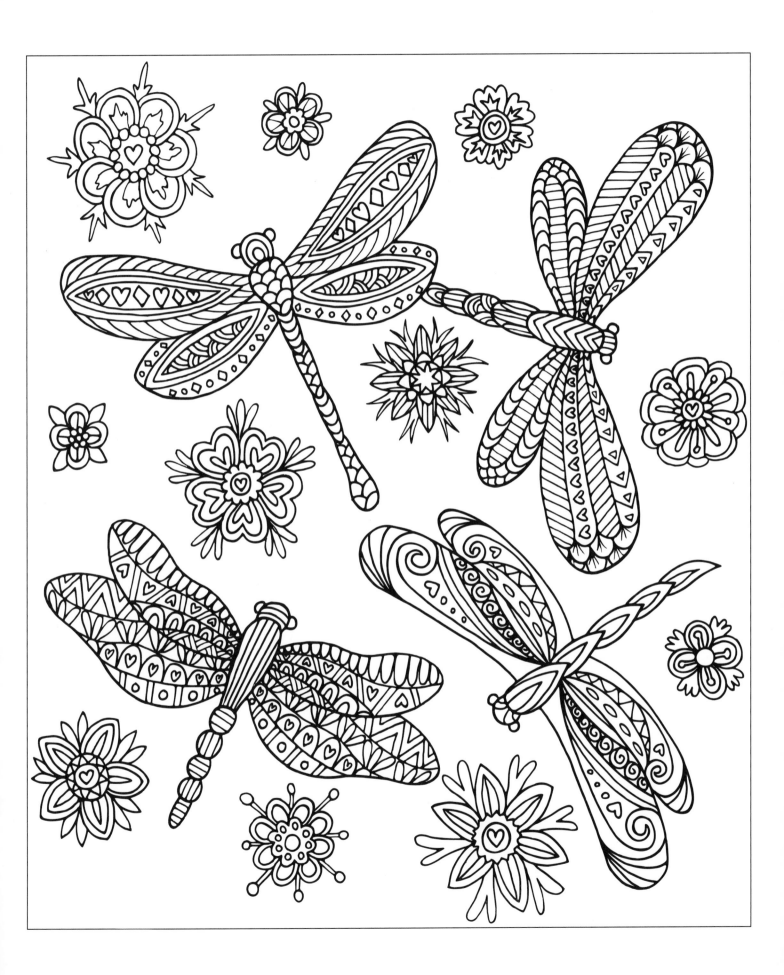

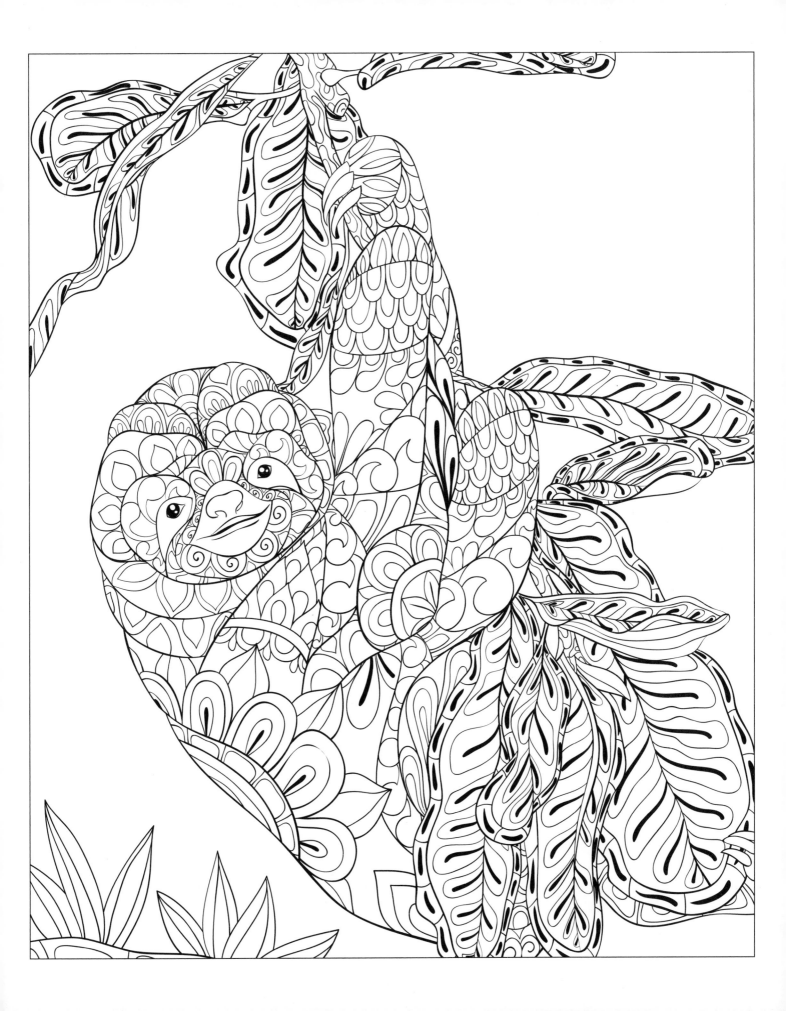